MICHELLE OBAMA
IN HER OWN WORDS

Edited by
Lisa Rogak

Published by Virgin Books 2009

4 6 8 10 9 7 5

Copyright © Lisa Rogak 2009

Published in the United States by PublicAffairs®, a member of the
Perseus Books Group

Lisa Rogak has asserted her right under the Copyright, Designs and Patents
Act 1988 to be identified as the author of this work

Designed by Ivelisse Robles Marrero
Text set in 10-point Cantoria MT

First published in Great Britain in 2009 by
Virgin Books
Random House, 20 Vauxhall Bridge Road,
London SW1V 2SA

www.virginbooks.com
www.rbooks.co.uk

Addresses for companies within The Random House Group Limited can be
found at: www.randomhouse.co.uk/offices.htm

The Random House Group Limited Reg. No. 954009

A CIP catalogue record for this book is available from the British Library

ISBN 9781905264858

The Random House Group Limited supports The Forest Stewardship
Council (FSC), the leading international forest certification organisation.
All our titles that are printed on Greenpeace-approved FSC-certified paper
carry the FSC logo.
Our paper procurement policy can be found at www.rbooks.co.uk/environment

Mixed Sources
Product group from well-managed
forests and other controlled sources
www.fsc.org Cert no. TT-COC-2139
© 1996 Forest Stewardship Council

Printed and bound in Great Britain by
CPI Mackays, Chatham ME5 8TD

To David Porter and John Willson

Introduction

NOW THAT BARACK OBAMA has become the forty-fourth president of the United States, the world is focused not only on what he will accomplish, but also on what kind of First Lady Michelle Obama will be. Throughout the long campaign season, Michelle Robinson Obama garnered a large amount of attention, kudos, and criticism about her words, actions, and even her appearance, but few people know what kind of role she'll play once she settles into the White House.

One clue is to examine her words and statements of the past. This volume aims to collect the most memorable of Michelle Obama's words for readers who are eager to learn more about America's new history-making First Lady. What is certain is that she's an incredibly accomplished woman in her own right, holding down high powered executive jobs in the Chicago mayor's office and at the University of Chicago. She was determined to follow a fast-track powerful career of her own years before she met the man who would become her husband. Some have said that while Barack has greater drive and ambition, Michelle possesses a more brilliant intelligence.

Despite her successes, she still tells anyone who asks that her most important job is mother to the presidential couple's two children. "My first job is going to continue to be mom-in-chief, making sure that in this transition, the girls are settled and that they know they will continue to be the center of our universe," she said only hours after the election.

Time will tell what role Michelle will play as First Lady. In the meantime, this book will help you to gain a clearer picture of this history-making woman.

Michelle Robinson Obama: A Brief Biography

MICHELLE LAVAUGHN ROBINSON was born on January 17, 1964, to Fraser Robinson, a city water plant employee, and Marian Shields, a secretary. She grew up in a one-bedroom apartment on Chicago's South Side, sharing a bedroom with her brother Craig, who was sixteen months older. People on the street often commented on the "twins."

Michelle's paternal great-great-grandfather, Jim Robinson, was a slave in South Carolina, and her grandfather moved to Chicago during the Great Migration of the early 1900s to escape the blatant racism of the South. Throughout her childhood, Michelle watched as white families left her inner-city neighborhood for a quieter life in the suburbs, known as the white flight of the 1960s and 1970s. Fraser and Marian instead turned their sole focus to helping their kids become well educated.

Michelle's natural intelligence was obvious very early. She learned to read by the age of four and skipped the second grade. By the sixth grade, she had enrolled in classes for gifted students, where she learned French and took accelerated courses, and she attended Whitney Young High School, the city's first magnet high school for gifted children. She was on the honor roll during all four years of high school, took advanced-placement classes, was a member of the National Honor Society, and graduated in 1981 as salutatorian of her class. Her future was bright.

After high school, Michelle attended Princeton University, graduating with a degree in sociology and cum laude honors in 1985. She attended Princeton during the height of the national debates over affirmative action. Her honors thesis was "Princeton-Educated Blacks and the Black Community." Michelle then went on to attend Harvard Law School and earned her JD in 1988. She was one year ahead of Barack Obama but didn't meet him until a year after she graduated.

After Harvard, Michelle accepted a position at Sidley Austin, a prestigious Chicago law firm. In 1989 she mentored a Harvard law student summer intern named Barack Obama. He asked her out, and she initially declined because she was his supervisor. But he was persistent and she was attracted to him, so she reluctantly gave in. On their first date, they saw the Spike Lee movie *Do the Right Thing*, after which he took her to a community organizing meeting. They married on October 18, 1992.

Shortly after the wedding, Michelle left the law firm and became executive director for Public Allies, a nonprofit leadership-training program in Chicago. Barack also worked for a community nonprofit while pursuing his political ambitions on the side. He was elected to the Illinois State Senate in 1996. That same year, Michelle became the associate dean of student services at the University of Chicago and developed the university's first community service program. She left to work in city government for a few years, taking a position as staff assistant to Chicago mayor Richard Daley and as Assistant Commissioner of Planning and Development.

Barack and Michelle waited almost seven years before having children. Their first daughter, Malia Ann, was born in 1999. Natasha (often called "Sasha") followed two years later in 2001.

Before the kids arrived, Barack and Michelle agreed that they would aspire to a dinner-together-every-night kind of life for their family. Once his political career took off, however, he spent many nights away from home, and his ideal family life fell by the wayside. This generated a certain amount of resentment for Michelle, who felt that her husband wasn't living up to his end of the bargain, and it created a good deal of friction between them for a couple of years. Michelle wondered what she'd gotten herself into. But once she recruited her mother and girlfriends to help out with the kids, the stress on both Barack and Michelle eased considerably, and their marriage settled down.

In Michelle's world, discipline reigns when it comes to her husband and her kids. Every day, she fills out to-do lists for Malia and

Natasha, making sure to schedule in time for play. Michelle is in bed most nights by 9:30 P.M. and rises each morning at 4:30 A.M. to work out for at least an hour.

To the casual observer, even to many friends, the Obamas' marriage is a bit of a mystery. While some say she wears the pants in the family—both have publicly admitted that he refers to her as "The Boss"—others say that it is an equal partnership, and that the presidency would not have been within reach if it weren't for Michelle.

In 2004, Barack Obama's star began to rise quickly with his keynote address at the Democratic National Convention when he was running for the U.S. Senate. His speech may have introduced him to the nation in one fell swoop, but it was Michelle's professional relationships that were vital to helping him win the election. He was supported by influential black business leaders, though overall they were closer to Michelle, because of her previous positions, than they were to him. When Barack won his seat in the U.S. Senate, she didn't pull back on the reins of her own ambitions. The couple decided it was best if he lived in Washington during the week and she remained in Chicago with the kids. After all, she was still dedicated to her own career; in May 2005, she became the Vice President of Community Relations and External Affairs at the University of Chicago Medical Center.

Initially, Michelle hated the idea of her husband's running for president. Not only did she not want the intrusiveness into her and her family's life that running for the highest office in the United States would bring, but she privately worried about the chance that some racist madman would tear her family apart with a single bullet. However, once the decision was made, Michelle fell into the task with a great passion, and she was fully committed to helping Barack win the nation's highest office.

MICHELLE OBAMA
IN HER OWN WORDS

The Quotes

ON AFRICAN AMERICANS

We are still struggling as a people with what is black.

Chicago Sun-Times, August 5, 2007

What minority communities go through still represents the challenges, the legacies, of oppression and racism. You know, when you
have cultures who feel like second-class citizens at some level, there's
this natural feeling within the community that we're not good enough,
that we can't be as smart or as prepared, and it's that internal struggle
that is always the battle.

New Yorker, March 10, 2008

One of the things I hope happens is that this country and this world
see yet another image of what it means to be black.

Chicago Tribune, April 22, 2007

We know what we need to do, but without that empathy, that core sense of mutual obligation, we don't get the right answers. We need that first, and then we can go through the issues that are affecting the Black community, from health care, to education, to an ineffective criminal justice system, to the dwindling of blue collar jobs. Everything that we are lacking as a society, right now today, is hitting the Black community hard. But we don't get to those answers until we get to our souls.

Chicago Defender, November 5, 2007

The thing that I worry most about is not what [the question if we're black enough] says about me and Barack. What does it say to our children? That somehow Michelle Obama is not black enough? Well, shoot, if I'm not black enough and Barack's not black enough, well, who are they supposed to be in this world?

Chicago Sun-Times, August 5, 2007

The black community has to shake off our fear because change doesn't happen without risk. Rosa Parks wasn't supposed to stay on that bus, and Martin Luther King wasn't supposed to speak out. We have a whole history of people who have taken risks far greater than anything that we're doing; this is nothing compared to the history we come from.

MSNBC, November 13, 2007

Black America will wake up and get it, but what we're dealing with in the black community is just the natural fear of possibility. The stuff that we see in these polls has played out my whole life. I've always been told by someone that I'm not ready, that I can't do something, my scores weren't high enough. There's always that doubt in the back of the minds of people of color, people who have been oppressed, that you believe that somehow someone is better than you. Inside you doubt that you can really do this because all you've been told is No. I would not be where I am, I wouldn't have gone to Princeton, I wouldn't have gone to Harvard, I certainly wouldn't be a practicing attorney, neither would Barack if we listened to that doubt.

MSNBC, November 13, 2007

As we've all said in the black community, we don't see all of who we are in the media. We see snippets and distortions of our community. So the world has this perspective that somehow Barack and Michelle Obama are different, that we're unique. And we're not. You just haven't seen us before.

Good Morning America, May 22, 2007

We've got to show people of color a different possibility. And I think that once they see what's possible, then they own it, they believe it.

MSNBC, November 13, 2007

The most important message we can send out is to show that we are a solid family with love and respect for one another. So many times you don't see that in the African American community.

Newsweek, January 28, 2008

ON AMERICA

This country is suffering from an empathy deficit. If you don't have it in you to be able to walk in another person's shoes, it's going to be difficult for us to move through these problems. What we need as a country is to start caring for one another in a very deep and fundamental way.

All Things Considered, NPR, July 9, 2007

Family in this country means different things. There are many different renditions of families and not all of them are recognized in ways that are successful.

Naperville Sun (IL), October 18, 2004

Divided . . . cynical . . . a nation that is just too mean. Mean has become a sport, a source for entertainment. We are a nation guided by fear. The problem with fear is that it clouds our judgment, it shuts us off.

Chicago Defender, December 10, 2007

ON AMERICANS

Despite any differences we may have, there is so much that unites us as Americans.

U.S. News & World Report, October 17, 2008

The American people can handle the truth. They just need to know what it looks like.

Boston Globe, February 21, 2008

It has been a blessing for us to have this opportunity to spend this year traveling the country. We've been in almost every state in this nation, in people's homes, in their kitchens, in their community centers, and just having the opportunity to be reminded of how decent the American people are and how our values are so closely linked, that gives me hope.

Ebony, September 2008

When people are worried about heat and gas and college they can't think clearly about immigration or race or gay and lesbian issues or our role in the war because people are afraid and they're panicked and they're subject to being manipulated by those who want to go a certain way, so I think when our country feels stable and whole again then hopefully we can talk honestly about what we really need to do to fix some of these broader issues.

MSNBC, November 13, 2007

ON BALANCING CAREER AND FAMILY

Every other month since I've had children I've struggled with the notion of "Am I being a good parent? Can I stay home? Should I stay home? How do I balance it all?" I have gone back and forth every year about whether I should work.

Washington Post, May 11, 2007

I realized that I needed to focus on what kept myself sane instead of looking to Barack to give me the answers and to help fulfill me. I need support. It doesn't always have to come from him, and I don't need to be angry because he can't give me the support.

USA Today, May 11, 2007

I've spent 20 months traveling around the country, having conversations with working women and families. I hear, how do I manage a career or a job, and ensure that my kids are healthy and have what they need, and make sure I'm not losing my mind in the process of juggling it all?

What I've found is that these families don't have the resources they need to make the balance work. It's very difficult to make this work if you don't have a strong family-leave policy.

Minneapolis Star Tribune, October 14, 2008

I separate my life so that when I am on the road, I am on the road. It's sort of like you are Batman. When you turn that off, you put that cape away.

Chicago Sun-Times, August 7, 2007

I can't do everything.

People, November 17, 2008

With the exception of life in the public eye, I'd say that my life now is really no different from many of yours. I say this often. I wake up every morning like most women in this room, wondering what minor miracle I have to pull off to get through my day.

Campaign speech, July 8, 2007

My ability to get through my day greatly depends upon the relationships that I have with women: my mother, my aunt, my girlfriends, my neighbors, the mothers in my children's school. I have this wonderful network of women where we rely upon one another for emotional and practical support. In these women I find a place of comfort and sanity and peace like no other. We ground one another.

Campaign speech, July 8, 2007

The only difference between me and every other woman that I know is that my challenges are publicized, and I'm doing this juggling in front of cameras.

Boston Globe, October 28, 2007

We are struggling with this notion of balance. I think that is what we are all facing as women, because we are overworked and we are overscheduled and we are juggling, and we are not getting enough support. There is a part of me that feels it's very therapeutic to be out on the road with other women and to say, Hey, you are not crazy; this is hard.

The Intelligencer, October 27, 2007

I think my generation of professional women are sort of waking up and realizing that we potentially may not be able to have it all, not at the same time.

Essence, September 2007

We all agonize about that work-family balance. We always feel like whatever we decided to do, we worry that it's the right thing to do, whether it's working part-time or staying at home. I think at every level women are racked with guilt and feel like they're not doing enough. I am no exception, and I can't say that I've completely resolved it.

Chicago Defender, November 5, 2007

If a toilet overflows, we're the ones frantically rescheduling the 9:00 A.M. meetings so that we can meet the plumber. And we have the added social pressure of being attractive, charming, and delightful mates, well-groomed, in good spirits, ready to be supportive of our significant others. I know I can get an amen on that. I'm tired just thinking about it.

All Things Considered, NPR, July 9, 2007

We try to convince ourselves that somehow doing it all is a badge of honor, but for many of us it is a necessity and we have to be very careful not to lose ourselves in the process.

Campaign speech, April 18, 2007

Every minute after I had my first child I questioned my decisions.

ABC News, January 24, 2008

I'm going to get tired. My hair is going to be messy.

Campaign speech, April 18, 2007

When you're growing up, you're taught, I am woman, hear me roar, I can do whatever I want to do. I guess you can, but there are serious tradeoffs in balancing and juggling. We have to be more honest with ourselves as women, particularly young women, to prepare them for the reality that there are difficult choices they have to make. It will be hard, it will be emotionally challenging and draining. It's not all pretty.

Concord Monitor (NH), December 6, 2007

People told me, "You can do it all. Just stay the course, get your education and you can raise a child, stay thin, be in shape, love your man, look good and raise healthy children." That was a lie.

Los Angeles Times, August 22, 2007

My mother says all the time, she doesn't know how [I] do it. And she means it.

Campaign speech, April 18, 2007

ON BARACK AS A FATHER

Barack has been on the road since our kids were born, and we treat that as a normal thing. They understand his schedule. Therefore, they thrive because we're happy about it. And if Mom is president, that's cool, as long as Dad or someone is going to their baseball games, is listening to their stories and their issues. There's got to be someone in a kid's life who makes them feel central.

Ladies' Home Journal, August 2008

Harry Potter is huge in our house. He handles all of that. Barack is the Harry Potter parent.

Associated Press (AP), July 18, 2007

It's a tough choice between, Do you stay for Malia's basketball game on Sunday or do you go to New Jersey and campaign for Corzine? Corzine got it this time around, but it's a constant pull to say, Hey, guys, you have a family here.

Chicago Tribune, December 25, 2005

Every day, his great desire is to be a better father. It touches me when our girls touch him. Whether it's with a story or a word. You can see it in his face. That's the leader I want: Somebody who is so moved by their own children, that they'll go out there and fight for everyone else's.

Ladies' Home Journal, August 2008

ON BARACK AS A ROCK STAR

He's had some attention in his life, and it's never gone to his head because we were raised with really pretty basic Midwestern values. It's who you are as a person and how you treat others that matters, not the degree you hold or the position you hold. All of this is very flattering, but he will not get a big head.

Arlington Heights Daily Herald (IL), July 27, 2004

What is interesting to me is when one of these stars is actually excited to see Barack. It's like, you're kidding, right? They are nervous, too! And I'm like, but you're Queen Latifah. Or Barbara Walters, coming up to me saying, I just want to introduce myself to you. I'm like, I know who you are.

Chicago Tribune, December 25, 2005

I'm kind of thrown by the reaction we're getting all over the country. Sometimes I wonder, you're all here for this guy? Barack Obama?

Concord Monitor (NH), May 5, 2007

Barack is not our savior. There are many of us who want to lay all of our wishes, fears and hopes at the feet of this young man, but life doesn't work that way and certainly politics doesn't work that way. You've got to be with him no matter what.

University Wire (UWire), October 26, 2004

ON BARACK'S CHOICE OF
JOE BIDEN AS VICE PRESIDENT

People ask, did I play a role? Absolutely not. I always tell him, this is your choice. You will be the President of the United States and you've got to have somebody that you can trust, that you think will have your back, who believes in you.

Gayle King Show, August 25, 2008

One thing a nominee earns is the right to pick the vice president that they think will best reflect their vision of the country, and I am just glad I will have nothing to do with it.

The View, June 18, 2008

ON BARACK'S CIGARETTE HABIT

To me it's a role model thing. You can smoke or you can be president.

Chicago Tribune, April 22, 2007

ON BARACK'S COLLEAGUES

You want people you can hang out with, that you trust, that you sit down and have a good conversation with, in addition to the advice, guidance and wisdom he brings. I think about it as a wife who's got to hang out with this crew, right?

People, September 8, 2008

ON BARACK'S HOUSEHOLD CHORES

When he comes home, he's taking out the garbage and he's doing the laundry and he's making up the beds, because the girls need to see him doing that, and he knows I need him to do that.

Vanity Fair, December 2007

When Barack's home he's going to be part of this life. He doesn't come home as the grand poobah.

Wall Street Journal, February 11, 2008

It matters less to me that Barack's the one helping with babysitting and giving me the time for myself; it's that I'm getting time.

People, June 18, 2007

ON BARACK'S SAFETY

Barack has Secret Service protection, and that in and of itself provides a level of security that didn't exist in our everyday lives. So I think that the question of security has been a bit overblown. We didn't make the decision to enter this worrying about safety. When you look at people who came before us, people like Martin Luther King Jr., there was a real reason to be afraid. We're living in different times. As far as I'm concerned, whatever we are sacrificing is nothing compared to what others have sacrificed.

U.S. News & World Report, February 1, 2008

I tell people something bad could happen, and I think about that. How could you not? But something great could happen as well.

Newsweek, January 28, 2008

We talk a lot as a family, and we keep our girls very much a part of the discussion when it comes to campaign planning. They're very comfortable with the Secret Service [assigned to our house]. They call them the Secret People.

Glamour, September 2007

We are grateful the Secret Service is a part of it. I'm probably more grateful than Barack, who loves to live a very normal life. This is the first sign that our lives aren't normal.

Newsweek, February 25, 2008

ON BARACK'S SHORTCOMINGS

The Barack Obama who lives in my house is not as impressive. He still has trouble putting his socks actually in the dirty clothes [hamper], and he still doesn't do a better job than Sasha at making his bed, so you'll have to forgive me if I'm a little stunned at this whole Barack Obama thing.

Associated Press (AP), May 29, 2007

[He] can't handle goody bags. Let me explain the goody bag thing. You have to go into the party store and choose the bags. Then you have to choose what to put in the bags, and what is in the boys' bags has to be different from what is in the girls' bags. You'd walk in there and wander around the aisles for an hour, and then your head would explode.

Michelle as quoted in Barack Obama, *The Audacity of Hope*

I'm a better dancer than he is.

Ellen Degeneres Show, September 8, 2008

ON BEING A MOTHER

At times it can be wearing, because you're on 24/7. Part of what we've had to figure out is what kind of support do I need to make my life less hectic? I'd like the support to come from Dad, but when it can't, I just really need the support. It doesn't really matter whether it's him or not as long as our kids are happy and they feel like they are connected to him. So I have to get over the fact that it's not him. It's Mom, friends, babysitters.

Chicago Tribune, December 25, 2005

My support for my husband comes straight from my motherhood bones.

ABC News, January 24, 2008

The days I stay home with my kids without going out, I start to get ill. My head starts to ache. I like to talk about it, because I think every couple struggles with these issues. People don't tell you how much kids change things. I think a lot of people give up on themselves. They get broken, but if we can talk about it, we can help each other.

The Telegraph (UK), July 26, 2008

The girls get into our bed and I turn on the lights so we're sort of waking up. And we talk. We talk about Daddy being President, about adolescence, about the questions they have.

People, August 4, 2008

The first priority is to make sure that my kids have their heads on straight. They are great and they are stable and they are confident, and I want to make sure that they stay that way.

Chicago Sun-Times, August 7, 2007

ON BEING COMPARED TO JACKIE ONASSIS

I'm flattered, not just because she was a style icon, but because she managed to raise some pretty sane and terrific kids in the midst of a lot of drama and difficulty.

Ebony, September 2008

Camelot to me doesn't work. It was a fairy tale that turned out not to be completely true because no one can live up to that. And I don't want to live like that.

USA Today, May 11, 2007

I had the honor to meet Caroline Kennedy. And to see her as such a decent, normal, healthy, whole and stable individual just makes me think even more of her mother for having been able to set the kind of tone in their life that has led them to be such fine adults. That's all I could ever hope for. That would be the greatest goal that I could ever live out, raising two beautiful decent human beings in my daughters.

Ebony, September 2008

ON HER CAREER PATH

Barack and I had both struggled with the question: When you know you've been blessed and know you have a set of gifts, how do you maximize those gifts so you're impacting the greatest number of people? And what do you do? Is it community organizing? Is it politics? Is it as a parent? Our answer at some level is it can be all of that.

Washington Post, November 28, 2007

Barack hasn't relied deeply on me for his career path, and I haven't relied on him at all for mine. I understand why people want to make sure that somehow I'm not using my husband's influence to build my career, and I haven't.

Chicago Tribune, April 22, 2007

I wanted to experience other fields. I thought it was too limiting to decide already that [a corporate law career] was [enough] for me.

Daily Princetonian, December 7, 2005

I looked out at my neighborhood and sort of had an epiphany that I had to bring my skills to bear in the place that made me. I wanted to have a career motivated by passion and not just money.

New York Times, June 18, 2008

I started thinking about the fact that I went to some of the best schools in the country and I have no idea what I want to do. That kind of stuff got me worked up because I thought, This isn't education. You can make money and have a nice degree. But what are you learning about giving back to the world, and finding your passion and letting that guide you, as opposed to the school you got into?

Newsweek, February 25, 2008

ON HER CHILDHOOD

What I learned growing up is that if I'm not going to get my butt kicked every day after school, I can't flaunt my intelligence in front of peers who are struggling with a whole range of things. So you've got to be smart without acting smart. [It's like] speaking two languages.

Chicago Sun-Times, September 19, 2004

I say this not to be modest, but there are so many young people who could be me. There's nothing magical about my background. I am not a super-genius. I had good parents and some good teachers and some decent breaks, and I worked hard. Every other kid I knew could have been me, but they got a bad break and didn't recover. It's like I tell the young people I talk to: the difference between success and failure in our society is a very slim margin. You almost have to have that perfect storm of good parents, self-esteem and good teachers.

The Telegraph (UK), July 26, 2008

I came into our marriage with a more traditional notion of what a family is. It was what I knew growing up—the mother at home, the father works, you have dinner around the table. I had a very stable, conventional upbringing, and that felt very safe to me.

Vanity Fair, December 2007

I was raised to believe I could do it all, and that was very empowering.

New York Times, August 28, 2008

When you have a parent with a disability [Michelle's father had multiple sclerosis], control and structure become critical habits, just to get through the day.

O, The Oprah Magazine, November 2007

I heard that growing up, "You talk like a white girl."

Chicago Tribune, April 22, 2007

I did exactly what leaders in my community told me to do. They said do your best in school, work hard, study, get into the best schools you can get into, and when you do that, baby, you bring that education back and you work in your communities.

Chicago Sun-Times, August 5, 2007

The life I had growing up seems so much more simple.

New Yorker, March 10, 2008

There's something that happens to you when you grow up regular.

Campaign speech, Akron, Ohio, October 24, 2008

The truth is, I'm not supposed to be standing here. I'm a statistical oddity. Black girl, brought up on the South Side of Chicago. Was I supposed to go to Princeton? No. They said maybe Harvard Law was too much for me to reach for. But I went, I did fine.

Newsweek, February 25, 2008

There were no miracles in my life. The thing that I saw that many of us still see is hard work and sacrifice.

Associated Press (AP), April 16, 2008

My lens of life, how I see the world, is through my background, my upbringing.

New Yorker, March 10, 2008

ON HER CHILDREN

Barack and I are always checking: *Are they still OK?* Every week, there's a gut check.

Glamour, September 2007

My children force me to keep my feet on the ground.

Newhouse News Service (NNS), August 10, 2008

Malia's [birthday is] the Fourth of July. Yes, we planned it that way. I cooperated. I was supposed to have her on July first, but I waited because my daughter would be more historic.

Associated Press (AP), June 13, 2008

They're living in a family where they've got an African American grandmother and an Indonesian aunt. They've got a Chinese American cousin. They've got African American cousins. They've got a multiracial cousin in Africa who's African and English. The in-laws of our in-laws, who are Chinese Canadian, are part of their families. Their world is bigger.

Ladies' Home Journal, August 2008

I believe that kids thrive with structure and rules and boundaries. I'm a big proponent of that. And I've been grateful that Barack supports that. So when he comes home after a long week away it's not like he's the fun dad who does all the fun and I do all the work. He definitely reinforces the rules that we have in place, and one of those is making bedtime. We have a pretty strict bedtime.

Larry King Live, October 8, 2008

I'm so happy that my girls will grow up where the prospect of a woman or African American president is normal. And that's one of the major reasons why our family has invested so much into this campaign. I want them to grow up in a world where they don't have to limit themselves, where they can dream and achieve without ever hitting a glass ceiling.

Momlogic.com, July 31, 2008

We don't want them to become political props.

Chicago Tribune, May 28, 2007

One thing I learned from Barack is there is not one right way to parent.

Washington Post, December 14, 2007

My girls are the first thing I think about when I wake up in the morning and the last thing I think about when I go to bed. When people ask me how I'm doing, I say, "I'm only as good as my most sad child."

New York Times, October 28, 2008

They break our hearts. And they have been so good about this process, and patient, and understanding. Kids will adjust to anything you throw at them. Our job is to not keep asking so much of them that they crack under the pressure.

Ladies' Home Journal, August 2008

We don't pull them out of their world.

Chicago Sun-Times, July 1, 2008

If I call in and there's something not right with them, my whole day is messed up.

Campaign speech, October 22, 2008

I want my girls to really be free, to reach and dream for whatever they can imagine. I don't want anybody telling them what they can't do. I want them to be proud to live in this country. I want them to be able to travel the world with pride. And I don't want that just for my girls, I want that for all of our children, and we're not there. We're not there.

Brattleboro Reformer (VT), December 6, 2007

My kids are having a good life. Do not worry about them. They're doing well.

Campaign speech, July 8, 2007

Our concern is that they stay normal. Where I gain comfort is that all of these [presidential] children have turned out to be pretty decent kids, even with the bumps and bruises that go along.

People, November 17, 2008

They are our hearts. They light up our lives. I don't care where I am, whether I'm on the campaign trail, at work, in a car, I'm worrying about their health and well-being. I want to make sure that they are happy and healthy and whole.

Campaign speech, October 7, 2008

ON HER COLLEGE YEARS

Being one of the school's few African American students at the time, I found there weren't many opportunities for minorities. So we created a community within a community and got involved at places like the Third World Center.

Daily Princetonian, December 7, 2005

The first time I set foot on Princeton, when I first got in I thought there's no way I can compete with these kids. I mean, I got in but I'm not supposed to be here. Then I get there and I thought these kids had the answers. The truth was that the toughest part of Princeton was getting in. Then I got into Harvard, and the more I achieved, the more I realized that they don't know any more than I do. They just believe in themselves in a way that's very different.

MSNBC, November 13, 2007

I remember being shocked by college students who drove BMWs. I didn't even know parents who drove BMWs.

The Telegraph (UK), July 26, 2008

The path I have chosen to follow by attending Princeton will likely lead to my further integration and/or assimilation into a white cultural and social structure that will only allow me to remain on the periphery of society, never becoming a full participant.

From her 1985 undergraduate thesis,
"Princeton Educated Blacks and the Black Community"

The thing about these wonderful schools is they can be surprisingly narrowing to your perspective. You can be a lawyer or you can work on Wall Street; those are the conventional options. They are easy, socially acceptable, and financially rewarding. Why wouldn't you do it?

The Telegraph (UK), July 26, 2008

Princeton University was really my first exposure to the possibility of the Ivy League. It wasn't that I couldn't get in, or I couldn't thrive, or I couldn't survive. I didn't know to want that. It wasn't the vision that I could see for myself because I couldn't see anybody around me doing that.

Los Angeles Times, August 22, 2007

I have found that at Princeton no matter how liberal and open-minded some of my white professors and classmates try to be toward me, I sometimes feel like a visitor on campus, as if I really don't belong.

> *From her 1985 undergraduate thesis,*
> *"Princeton Educated Blacks and the Black Community"*

I gave up the notion of being a pediatrician after I realized that organic chemistry was going to be [required]. I don't think I have put my heart and soul into the notion of being a lawyer.

> *U.S. News & World Report,* February 1, 2008

Unfortunately, there are very few adequate support groups which provide some form of guidance and counsel for Black students having difficulty making the transition from their home environments to Princeton's environment. Most students are dependent upon the use of their own faculties to carry them through Princeton.

> *From her 1985 undergraduate thesis,*
> *"Princeton Educated Blacks and the Black Community"*

When I wasn't studying, I was working.

> *Daily Princetonian,* December 7, 2005

ON HER CRITICS

One of the lessons that I grew up with was to always stay true to yourself and never let what somebody else says distract you from your goals. And so when I hear about negative and false attacks, I really don't invest any energy in them, because I know who I am.

Marie Claire, October 2008

I take them in my stride. It's part of this process and we are not new to politics.

The View, June 18, 2008

Throughout my life I have not paid much attention to what people say about me who don't know me.

All Things Considered, NPR, August 25, 2008

You couldn't be in politics if you didn't have a thick skin. There are people who say things. This race just isn't about me and Barack. It's about something bigger.

Larry King Live, October 8, 2008

Somehow I've been caricatured as this emasculating wife. Barack and I laugh about that. It's just that do you think anyone could emasculate Barack Obama? Really now.

Newsweek, February 25, 2008

I don't listen to a lot of it. I tune out.

Chicago Defender, January 30, 2008

I need stability and evenness, and not paying attention to media coverage helps. It's usually either really, really good or really, really bad, which doesn't reflect what people are thinking.

Newhouse News Service (NNS), August 10, 2008

You are amazed sometimes at how deep the lies can be. I mean, "Whitey"? That's something that George Jefferson would say. Anyone who says that doesn't know me. They don't know the life I've lived. They don't know anything about me.

New York Times, June 18, 2008

Surprisingly, it does not really affect me as an individual.

Sunday Telegraph London, December 23, 2007

We've developed a thick skin along the way. When you're out campaigning, there will always be criticism. I just take it in stride, and at the end of the day, I know that it comes with the territory.

Momlogic.com, July 31, 2008

If I wilted every time somebody in my life mischaracterized me or called me a bad name, I would have never finished Princeton, would have never gone to Harvard, and wouldn't be sitting here with him. So these are the lessons we want to teach our kids. You know who you are, so what anybody else says is just interesting fodder.

Essence, September 2008

ON DATING BARACK

I've got nothing in common with this guy, [I thought]. He grew up in Hawaii! Who grows up in Hawaii? He was biracial. I was like, okay, what's that about? And then it's a funny name, Barack Obama. Who names their child Barack Obama?

Washington Post, November 28, 2007

I lowered my expectations because I thought this was probably just a black man who can talk straight. I did what most people do, I made assumptions based on the bio. Then I found out that he was biracial. I didn't know what to do with that.

O, The Oprah Magazine, November 2007

His first car had so much rust that there was a rusted hole in the passenger door. You could see the ground when you were driving by. He loved that car. It would shake ferociously when it would start up. I thought, "This brother is not interested in ever making a dime." I would just have to love him for his values.

Washington Post, October 5, 2008

I told him if this isn't leading to marriage, then, you know, don't waste my time.

Chicago Sun-Times, September 19, 2004

We had many debates about how to best [bring about] change. We both wanted to affect the community on a larger scale than either of us could individually, and we wanted to do it outside of big corporations. It was not a "make a lot of money, wrap it up and call it a day" thing.

Daily Princetonian, December 7, 2005

I found him to be charming and funny and self-deprecating, and he was very serious but he didn't take himself too seriously.

USA Today, May 11, 2007

When I first met him, I fell in deep like.

Good Housekeeping, November 2008

We went to a reception and Spike Lee was there, and Barack told him, "I owe you a lot." Spike Lee got a big kick that *Do the Right Thing*, as Barack said, "got him a little play" because in the movie I allowed him to touch my knee.

Chicago Sun-Times, September 19, 2004

I wasn't expecting much. Any black guy who spent his formative years on an island had to be a little nerdy, a little strange.

Washington Post, May 11, 2007

To see him transform himself from the guy who was a summer associate in a law firm with a suit and then come into this church basement with folks who grew up like me, but who were challenged and struggling in ways that I never would, and to take off that suit and tie and become a whole other person and connect with people in the same way he had connected with folks in that firm, you don't see someone who can make that transition and do it comfortably. To feel comfortable in his own skin and to touch people's hearts in the way that he did, [well], people connected with his message. And I knew then and there there's something different about this guy.

CBS Evening News with Katie Couric, February 15, 2008

His wardrobe was kind of cruddy. He had five shirts and seven blue suits and a bunch of ties. He looks good in his clothes because he is tall and thin, but he has never been into clothes. I had to really tell him to get rid of the white jacket.

Washington Post, October 5, 2008

ON THE DECISION TO RUN FOR PRESIDENT

I thought, "Uhhhh, you're kidding!" It was like, "No, not right now, right?" There was a period of Let's not do this now, let's press the easy button! Can we get a break, please?

Vanity Fair, December 2007

I'm one of these people who walks down every dark road before I take on a pretty ambitious process. And that's one of the things that I did. I thought through all the things that could go wrong. So I kind of prepared myself. And what I found is that there hasn't been anything that I didn't expect to happen.

Larry King Live, February 11, 2008

The selfish part of me says, "Run away! Just say no!" because my life would be better. But that's the problem we face as a society, we have to stop making the *Me* decision and we have to make the *We* and *Us* decision.

Washington Post, November 28, 2007

I took off the Michelle Obama hat, the selfish hat, the one that says "No," and put on my citizen hat, my hopeful hat, and realized that I want Barack Obama to lead me, even if it's inconvenient. We have to be bold.

Salon.com, November 28, 2007

Honestly, the last thing that I wanted for my girls was to have them grow up in this, have their lives turned upside down in the midst of all of this, to have them hear their parents being criticized on national TV.

Chicago Tribune, July 28, 2008

ON DISAGREEMENTS WITH BARACK

We fight over the remote. He likes to click back and forth to the sports channel. And if I'm clicking, I'm clicking back and forth to HGTV. So it just depends who gets there first.

Rocky Mountain News, July 17, 2008

We're two well-versed lawyers who know each other really well. We each think we're right about everything, and can argue each other into a corner.

Wall Street Journal, February 11, 2008

There was a meeting of the minds that [Barack and I] had to reach. I wasn't content with saying, "You're doing important things in the world, so go off and be important and I'll handle everything else here [at home]." Because the truth is, if I did that, I'd probably still be angry.

Vanity Fair, December 2007

The big thing I figured out was that I was pushing to make Barack be something I wanted him to be for me. I believed that if only he were around more often, everything would be better. So I was depending on him to make me happy. Except it didn't have anything to do with him. I needed support. I didn't necessarily need it from Barack.

O, The Oprah Magazine, November 2007

I tease him all the time. Today, he still didn't put the butter up after he made his breakfast. I was like, You're just asking for it, you know that I am giving a speech, why don't you just put the butter up? He said he was just giving me material.

Campaign speech, April 18, 2007

You want to know how Barack prepares for a debate? He hangs out with me, and he's ready.

New York Times, October 28, 2008

ON DISCIPLINING HER KIDS

There are downstairs rules, different rules in different parts of the house.

People, August 4, 2008

No whining, arguing, or annoying teasing.

People, August 4, 2008

ON DIVERSITY

I hate diversity workshops. Real change comes from having enough comfort to be really honest and say something very uncomfortable.

New York Times, June 18, 2008

Diversity can't be taken care of with ten kids. There is an isolation that comes with that.

New York Times, June 18, 2008

ON THEIR ECONOMIC STRUGGLES

The only reason we're not in debt today is because Barack wrote two best-selling books. That's like hitting the Lotto, because that was not a solid financial plan.

Chicago Tribune, April 19, 2008

I remember those days clearly, that collection agency, the loan debt people calling you telling you that you've got a few more days before you're in trouble.

Chicago Tribune, April 19, 2008

ON HER EDUCATION

Many people wouldn't think that someone with my background would end up where I am. . . . No one talked to me about Princeton or Harvard, or even going to college.

Herald News (Joliet, IL), October 14, 2004

I like kids, and I thought being a doctor was a noble profession. But then I got to high school and started taking science. And math.

Reader's Digest, October 2008

You get the best education you can get, you work hard, you bring that education back and you give back, and you push the next generation to be better.

MSNBC, November 13, 2007

Most kids like me didn't try, they said okay, you're probably right, I wasn't ready [for Princeton or Harvard]. There's probably some magical thing I didn't get because I'm black or I'm poor or I'm a girl or I'm not pretty enough.

Concord Monitor (NH), December 6, 2007

If my future were determined just by my performance on a standardized test, I wouldn't be here. I guarantee you that.

Campaign speech, February 18, 2008

ON THE ELITIST TAG

I find it funny that people have tried to label Barack as an elitist. This is the man who grew up not knowing his father, with a young, single mother who he watched struggle to make ends meet, even going on food stamps at one point. And despite the economic struggles that his family went through, Barack turned down lucrative careers on Wall Street and went to work in communities to help folks in need on the South Side of Chicago, helping families who'd been devastated when the local steel plants shut down.

Marie Claire, October 2008

I am a product of a working-class background; I am one of those folks who grew up in that struggle. So when people talk about this elitist stuff, I say, you couldn't possibly know anything about me.

Associated Press (AP), April 16, 2008

I'm still waiting for Barack's trust fund to show up.

Evansville Courier & Press (IN), April 17, 2008

ON EXERCISE

Exercise is really important to me. So if I'm ever feeling tense or stressed or like I'm about to have a meltdown, I'll put on my iPod and head to the gym or out on a bike ride along Lake Michigan with the girls.

Marie Claire, October 2008

For me, exercise is more than just physical—it's therapeutic.

Momlogic.com, July 31, 2008

[Being fit] has become even more important as I've had children, because I'm also thinking about how I'm modeling health to my daughters. I'm trying to teach my daughters moderation and constancy, that exercise is not a luxury, it is a necessity.

Ebony, September 2008

My workout routine is 90 minutes long, and I do it up to four times a week, depending on my travel schedule. It includes cardio, free weights, treadmill, stair-walking and other activities.

Chicago Sun-Times, July 1, 2008

ON HER FAMILY

Family is first for us and it will always be that way,

Boston Globe, October 28, 2007

We've always been the kind of people who go to the soccer games, shop at Target, go for bike rides and make sure the girls get to the sleepovers they've been invited to. We still do that, but we usually have a lot of people watching now.

Newhouse News Service (NNS), August 10, 2008

ON FAMILY TIME

We spend time with other families and play games. Uno is a favorite game. We watch movies, the kids like *American Idol*, *SpongeBob*, and the Disney Channel. Barack likes action movies and I like romantic comedies. Barack loves *The Wire* but we were also *Sex and the City* fans when it was on. *The Sopranos* was one of our favorites. That's an example of an intense, gritty, long-term series you have to keep up with. He likes that kind of stuff.

Rocky Mountain News, July 17, 2008

We have just some of the most wonderful times when we visit Barack's grandmother in Hawaii. Those are always wonderful times, warm weather, a time to be together and laugh, when everybody's relaxed, no schedules, no nothing, just a lot of good fun together.

U.S. News & World Report, February 1, 2008

When it comes to family TV and movie time, what the girls say goes. We love to watch *The Incredibles*, *Shrek*, *Harry Potter*, and *Hannah Montana* together. But the girls will tell you, they only get an hour of television time each day, after their homework is finished.

Momlogic.com, July 31, 2008

We love to go to movies. It's all kid-centered. We've seen every kid's movie out. Haven't seen a grown-up movie since *Dreamgirls.*

Jet, September 2007

ON FAMILY VALUES

We have spent the last decade talking a good game about family values, but I haven't seen much evidence that we value women or family values. You can't just tell a family of four to suck it up and make it work.

ABC News, May 22, 2007

I think it's a unit that raises a child. In this couple, Barack is the person who has the skill, the inclination, the desire, the ability, to be in politics. I have no desire. So that's a good thing, in my view, since someone has to be focusing on the kids, and that's me. But it could easily be him. There's no reason why the nurturing has to come from Mom—it just has to be there.

Ladies' Home Journal, August 2008

ON HER FASHION SENSE

You can get some good stuff online.

Associated Press (AP), October 28, 2008

I found ways to pin my hair and tie it down and I deal with it. If it's not where it needs to be I pull it back. I just said I am not going to let hair be the dictator of my health.

Ebony, September 2008

I still go to Target. I do my own shopping.

Boston Globe, October 28, 2007

I love girly makeup and stuff, but my view is that's a lot of work. I want people to get used to my face more naturally so that I don't have to do that every day. Who's got time to put eyelashes on and all that?

Chicago Sun-Times, August 7, 2007

I do think that what you wear is a reflection of who you are. I love to look glamorous when there's a wonderful, purposeful event that is appropriate. But when I'm in Iowa campaigning with the girls, I am in Gap shorts and a T-shirt.

Ebony, September 2008

How she handles her hair: Headbands. I try not to do anything additional, because with black folks and perms, that's where your hair's on your pillow. So I tend to just slick it back.

Glamour, September 2007

I can be comfortable in anything.

The Telegraph (UK), July 26, 2008

It's fun to look pretty.

The View, June 18, 2008

Wear what you like.

Chicago Sun-Times, July 1, 2008

I'm 5'11", so typically, I'm in flats. They're much better for keeping up with the girls and the pace of the campaign trail.

Marie Claire, October 2008

I stopped wearing pantyhose a long time ago because it was painful and they'd always rip. And I'm 5-foot-11 so I'm tall—nothing fits. Put 'em on, rip 'em. It's just inconvenient.

The View, June 18, 2008

While I love fashion, I don't have a lot of time to think about it. That is really my style: some really nice stuff for special occasions, but a whole lot of stuff you can throw on and wash, and it can get dirty, and you don't lose your mind because you got a spot on it.

Rocky Mountain News, July 17, 2008

ON HER FATHER

My Dad was our rock.

One Nation speech, Democratic National Convention,
August 25, 2008

You never wanted to disappoint him. We would be bawling.

Newsweek, February 25, 2008

He and my mom poured everything they had into me and Craig. It was the greatest gift a child could receive: Never doubting for a single minute that you're loved and cherished and have a place in this world.

One Nation speech, Democratic National Convention,
August 25, 2008

ON FEEDING HER FAMILY

You can't just make a dinner. It's got to be a nutritious dinner, grown with good, fresh clean food. That takes time. Trust me. It is a message that we have talked about more and more in our household.

Chicago Tribune, July 28, 2008

Over the last year we shifted to organic. We started looking through our cabinets and reading the labels and realized there's high-fructose corn syrup in everything. Now we keep a bowl of fresh fruit in the house. But you have to go to the fruit stand a couple of times a week to keep that fruit fresh; a six-year-old won't eat the pruney grape or the brown banana. It's got to be fresh for them to want it. Who's got time to go to the fruit stand?

New Yorker, March 10, 2008

At country fairs: Stuff on a stick. Corn dogs and candied apples.

New Yorker, March 10, 2008

Cooking isn't one of my huge things.

Washington Post, May 11, 2007

We're bacon people.

The View, June 18, 2008

ON FEMINISM

I'm not that into labels. So if you laid out a feminist agenda, I would probably agree with a large portion of it. But I wouldn't identify as a feminist just like I probably wouldn't identify as a liberal or a progressive.

Washington Post, May 11, 2007

We all know our country's journey toward equality isn't finished yet. We have more work to do.

Associated Press (AP), August 27, 2008

I know that the life I'm living is still out of the reach of too many women. Too many little black girls. I don't have to tell you this. We know the disparities that exist across this country, in our schools, in our hospitals, at our jobs and on our streets.

Newsweek, January 28, 2008

ON HER "FIRST TIME I'M PROUD ABOUT AMERICA" QUOTE

The full quote: What we've learned over this year is that hope is making a comeback. It is making a comeback. And let me tell you something, for the first time in my adult lifetime, I'm really proud of my country. And not just because Barack has done well, but because I think people are hungry for change. And I have been desperate to see our country moving in that direction and just not feeling so alone in my frustration and disappointment. I've seen people who are hungry to be unified around some basic common issues, and it's made me proud.

Campaign speech, February 18, 2008

What I was clearly talking about was that I'm proud of how Americans are engaging in the political process. For the first time in my lifetime, I'm seeing people rolling up their sleeves in a way that I haven't seen and really trying to figure this out, and that's the source of pride that I was talking about.

Los Angeles Times, February 21, 2008

So let me tell you something. I am proud. I'm proud of this country, and I'm proud of the fact that people are ready to roll [and] do something phenomenal. I know I wouldn't be standing here—Barack and I, our stories wouldn't be possible—if it weren't for our fundamental belief and pride in this country and what it stands for.

Boston Globe, February 21, 2008

ON THE FIST BUMP

I'm not that hip. I got this from the young staff. That's the new high-five. It's now my signature bump.

The View, June 18, 2008

ON THE FUTURE

The changes that we need to make in this country are gonna be hard, and they're gonna require a whole lot of sacrifice from every single American. And it's gonna require a level of unity in this country that we haven't seen yet and we haven't experienced it, at least in my adult lifetime.

CBS Evening News with Katie Couric,
February 15, 2008

Things aren't going to get better when you wish for it or you hope for it: Things get better when regular folks take action to make change happen from the bottom up. Every major, historical moment in our time it has been made by folks who said, "Enough," and they banded together to move this country forward—and now is one of those times.

Speech, Georgetown, S.C., January 14, 2008

ON GETTING A DOG

[The girls'] main concern about this whole race was whether or not they could get a dog, that was the bargaining chip. It's like, "You want to run for president, we're getting a dog." And let me tell you we talk about that dog every day. What breed, how big, how small. Yesterday morning we talked about names. I said, "Look, you are getting a dog, just knock it off."

Chicago Sun-Times, May 14, 2008

ON HER GREAT-GREAT-GRANDFATHER,
A SLAVE

It's good to be a part of playing out history in this way. It could be anybody. But it's us, it's our family, it's that story, that's going to play a part in telling a bigger story. It is a process, of uncovering the shame, digging out the pride that is part of that story, so that other folks feel comfortable about embracing the beauty and the tangled nature of the history of this country.

Washington Post, October 2, 2008

An important message in this journey is that we're all linked through our histories of growth and survival in this country. Somewhere there was a slave owner—or a white family in my great-great-grandfather's time that gave him a place, a home, that helped him build a life—that again led to me. So who were those people? I would argue they're just as much a part of my history as my great-great-grandfather.

Washington Post, October 2, 2008

ON HEALTH CARE

It's mutual responsibility. Whatever health-care solution we bring to the table, people have to use it. People have to put good food in their bodies. People have to take their medication as directed. People can't sit and completely blame outside forces.

Chicago Tribune, April 22, 2007

How do we make sure our policies are structured in a way that supports balance, whether it's more work/family leave, or whether it's better health care? There are a lot of policies that go along with allowing women that freedom.

Ebony, September 2008

ON HILLARY CLINTON

No one has been more gracious and more helpful to me.

New York Times, August 28, 2008

My husband is a better candidate because of her. My daughters will think of themselves differently because of her. She has been nothing but gracious and open and warm and generous in this effort.

Chicago Tribune, July 28, 2008

Hillary has been phenomenal. From the minute after this was done, she has always been just cordial and open. I've called her. I've talked to her. She's given me advice about the kids. We've talked at length about this kind of stuff, how you feel, how you react. She has been amazing. She is a real pro and a woman with character.

Larry King Live, October 8, 2008

I'm sure there are some [similarities]. But I feel like I am uniquely me.

CBS Evening News with Katie Couric, February 15, 2008

I've always admired what she has been able to do with Chelsea. You can tell from one conversation with Chelsea that she's a mature, decent, well-balanced young lady. [The Clintons] did something right. Hillary talked about how they were very protective of her personal space, and how they created some real clear hard boundaries that were never crossed. That went a long way to retaining some normalcy for her.

Newsweek, November 5, 2008

I think the world of Hillary Clinton, particularly as a woman, having watched her go through a lot of what I might be going through and doing it with a level of grace, and raising a phenomenal daughter. There's no way that I would say absolutely not to one of the most successful and powerful and groundbreaking women on this planet.

International Herald Tribune, May 20, 2008

She is smart and gracious and everything she appears to be in public. Someone who's managed to raise what appears to be a solid, grounded child.

Chicago Magazine, October 2004

She has been completely forthcoming. She will spend as much time as I need on the phone. She's been completely gracious with her time and her advice, and I am grateful to her for that.

Newsweek, November 5, 2008

ON HER HUSBAND

I'm married to a man who gets it.

Campaign speech, October 22, 2008

Can his mind be changed?
Absolutely. Hey, I change it every day.

Larry King Live, February 11, 2008

He's a good man. First of all, he's my best friend. He's a phenomenal support to me and the girls. I mean this is a guy who, in the midst of this race, hasn't missed a parent/teacher conference. This is the stuff that I look at. He took the girls trick or treating. He came home for a day to buy the Christmas tree. He took me out for our anniversary. I mean, he is just consistent. But he *is* consistent. It's just his character, you know?

Larry King Live, February 11, 2008

I listen very intently when he speaks because I always want to find out whether I believe it, you know, whether I feel that authenticity. And I do every single time he speaks, but there are just some times when he touches my heart in a way that makes me very clear about why we're doing this.

MSNBC, November 13, 2007

Barack is one of the few men I've met who is not intimidated by strong women. He relishes the fact that I'm not impressed by him.

Chicago Tribune, April 22, 2007

The one thing that I can tell people is that Barack has not disappointed me once in the twenty years or more that I've known him. Not once. And that's the only reason why I can be sitting here.

Gayle King Show, August 25, 2008

Barack gets angry. It's not something that's said about him, he can take any name-calling or the back-and-forth, but it's the unfairness that we're seeing across the country that makes him mad.

Larry King Live, October 8, 2008

He's got me, he's got my mom, he's got our girls. He's surrounded [by women] and he loves it. He's very comfortable with women, and he's comfortable with women who push him. That's the only reason I could be married to him. It's the only reason it would work.

Rocky Mountain News, July 17, 2008

He's a gifted man, but in the end, he's just a man.

Chicago Tribune, April 22, 2007

The Barack Obama I know today is the same man I fell in love with nineteen years ago. He's the same man who drove me and our new baby daughter home from the hospital ten years ago this summer, inching along at a snail's pace, peering anxiously at us in the rearview mirror, feeling the whole weight of her future in his hands.

> One Nation speech, Democratic National Convention,
> August 25, 2008

[I know he's stressed] when he's writing small notes late at night. When he's really sort of brooding about something, it's late at night, and there's a lot of little note-writing going on.

> *Ladies' Home Journal*, August 2008

My best accessory.

> *Ebony*, September 2008

Barack is exactly who he appears to be. I know that's hard to understand in politics. He's smart, he's decent, a good husband and a good father.

> *Reno Gazette-Journal (NV)*, August 10, 2007

ON HER HUSBAND'S
PRESIDENTIAL ABILITIES

He is incredibly smart and he is very able to deal with a strong woman, which is one of the reasons he can be president, because he can deal with me.

Good Morning America, May 22, 2007

You see people who can live well in corporate America. They can wear that uniform well. They can't make the transition and vice versa. Barack lived comfortably in those two worlds.

CBS Evening News with Katie Couric, February 15, 2008

Barack is going to make mistakes. But, see, the beauty of Barack making mistakes is that he's not going to be so stubborn that he can't admit that he's making mistakes and he can't look at another way of approaching things.

Larry King Live, February 11, 2008

You will not see another politician like [Barack] in your lifetime. Because they don't come along very often. There are other people like him out there, but they don't choose to go into politics because they have sense. My husband is a little crazy.

Salon.com, November 28, 2007

He's not just going to tell you what you think you want to hear.

Larry King Live, February 11, 2008

And he has to continue to make [his children] a priority even as he's the leader of the free world. I think that's an important thing for him to model for others. It's this notion that if *he* can do it, then we all have to really fight for it.

Newsweek, November 5, 2008

He is going to demand that you shed your cynicism. That you put down your divisions. That you come out of your isolation, that you move out of your comfort zones. That you push yourselves to be better. And that you engage. Barack will never allow you to go back to your lives as usual, uninvolved, uninformed.

Worcester Telegram & Gazette (MA), May 29, 2008

If he's doing his job, he's going to say things that you don't agree with.

USA Today, May 11, 2007

When was the last time we've had a president of the United States who spent years working on the streets in a major city, for years working with people who never had a voice and advocating for better streets, cleaner streets, safer communities?

CBS Evening News with Katie Couric, February 15, 2008

I married him because I saw that specialness.

Concord Monitor (NH), May 5, 2007

ON HOW HER FAMILY'S
LIVES WILL CHANGE

In the end you have to prioritize your life around your children so that they know that they continue to be the most important people in the world to you even if you are possibly going to be the next president of the United States.

Tell Me More, NPR, January 25, 2008

It will be a hard transition for those little girls. They'll be going on eleven and eight. They'll be leaving the only home that they've known. Someone's got to be the steward of that transition. And it can't be the President of the United States. It will be me.

Ladies' Home Journal, August 2008

We certainly don't want to spend the next four or eight years in the White House trying to live up to a persona that isn't true. I want to be able to be me, and we're certainly not going to change just to win. Because the point isn't winning, it's changing the country, its changing America, it's changing the way you live. It's throwing this game out, shaking it up and throwing it out the window, and not just playing it better than the people who played it before.

MSNBC, November 13, 2007

As first lady, my number one job would still be Mom. At seven and ten, our daughters are young. If we move to Washington, my first priority will be to ensure they stay grounded and healthy, with normal childhoods—including homework, chores, dance, and soccer.

U.S. News & World Report, October 17, 2008

Our hope is that we do some of what we've been doing for the last year and a half. That we really treat our family life as separate as you can, that we keep the girls' lives very set apart from this whole experience. Which means we have to just pretend like this isn't happening. And we've gotten sort of good at it. It'll be a little bit more challenging, but I think that staying connected to friends and family who know you [will help].

Newsweek, November 5, 2008

It's just more of the same, except more people are watching. I think that if you're secure in yourself and you sort of know who you are— not to say we don't have anything else to learn but, you know, we're pretty grounded—that helps you handle all of the ups and downs of this kind of stuff.

Larry King Live, February 11, 2008

ON HOW SHE DEALS WITH STRESS

Our high stress levels and busy lives also make it difficult for us to be completely on point mentally. We've not yet embraced the notion that it's OK for us to take time out for ourselves, to find the time to be still, to be quiet and to reflect on our lives. I know I can't do it. You know, the minute my kids go to bed at 8:30—click, click, the TV. And I need time to wind down and to just reflect.

Campaign speech, July 8, 2007

ON HOW SHE INFLUENCES BARACK

I don't spend any time at all, because I don't have the time, to dig deep into his energy policy. It's not my forte, I'm not an energy person, I'm not necessarily the one who has particularly interesting insight [in that area].

MSNBC, November 13, 2007

The notion of sitting around the table with a set of policy advisors—no offense—makes me yawn. I like creating stuff.

Ladies' Home Journal, August 2008

ON HOW SHE MAKES DECISIONS

Life changes and I never see one set of decisions as permanent. I look at it as this is what I'm doing for this time and make sense at this time in my life and I don't try to predict what the future will hold in terms of those types of decisions.

Chicago Defender, November 5, 2007

ON IMMIGRATION

We would have an immigration policy that brings 12 million people out of the shadows.

Associated Press (AP), August 27, 2008

ON THEIR IMAGE AS A COUPLE

We are new to politics in terms of just this approach—how we talk, how we look—imagine having a president of the United States who is just two years out of college debt and understands that.

Brattleboro Reformer (VT), December 6, 2007

You've never seen anyone like us before, and that's a little freaky, isn't it? It's like, "They're real!" Well, guess what? Real people can be politicians too. We as a country have grown suspicious of real. We take the fake.

Salon.com, November 28, 2007

ON IRAQ

Instead of putting millions into a war, we could be providing universal health care. Instead of putting millions into a war, we could be expanding education and increasing the quality of education for all children. Instead of putting money into a war, we could be providing better quality childcare.

All Things Considered, NPR, July 9, 2007

You can't do the *I told you so*. We're in a war. We have young men and women over there fighting right now, and we have to think pragmatically about bringing this to an end. That's the conversation now. That was then, this is now. We have to deal with Iraq today is what he has been saying. And, again, you can't take a rash approach. You can't just pull folks out. You can't just cut off funding completely. You've got to unravel this thing in a common sense way.

Good Morning America, May 22, 2007

ON LAURA BUSH

Laura Bush was just so gracious. She is a really sweet person and couldn't have been more excited and enthusiastic about the tour [of the White House]. So that was wonderful. And her entire team, their team has been working closely just to make us feel welcome.

60 Minutes, November 16, 2008

That's what I like about Laura Bush. [She has] a calm, rational approach to these issues. And you know, I'm taking some cues. I mean, there's a balance.

The View, June 18, 2008

There's a reason people like her. It's because she doesn't, you know, add fuel to the fire.

New York Times, June 19, 2008

ON HER LAW CAREER

Work is rewarding. I love losing myself in a set of problems that have nothing to do with my husband and children. Once you've tasted that, it's hard to walk away.

The Telegraph (UK), July 26, 2008

I had a fancy office, a secretary, and a new Saab. But it wasn't enough.

Joliet Herald News (IL), October 14, 2004

I didn't see a whole lot of people who were just thrilled to be there. I met people who thought this was a good life. But were people waking up just bounding out of bed to get to work? No.

Newsweek, February 25, 2008

I could die tomorrow. I had to ask myself, is this how I want to spend my time? I knew I would never feel a sense of passion or joy about the law. I was on a conveyor belt. Law school had just been the next step.

The Telegraph (UK), July 26, 2008

ON HER LEGACY

I think we're gonna sort of tip the scales of balance in favor of most Americans. I believe we'll have universal health care, I believe that we'll have more of a chance of people's wages keeping up with the cost of living, I think we're going to have a presidency that is serious about global warming, that is going to begin to talk openly about the challenges we face.

MSNBC, November 13, 2007

ON LIFE IN THE WHITE HOUSE

The White House is beautiful. It is awe-inspiring. It is a great gift and an honor to be able to live here. And, you know, we want to make sure that we're upholding what that house stands for. But I couldn't help but envisioning the girls running into their rooms and, you know, running down the hall, with a dog. And, you know, you start picturing your life there. And our hope is that the White House will feel open and fun and full of life and energy.

60 Minutes, November 16, 2008

Barack was gone [from home] most of an entire two-year period. And now, we get to be together under the one roof, having dinners together. And, you know, I envision the kids coming home from school and being able to run across the way to the Oval Office and see their dad before they start their homework. And having breakfast. And he'll be there to tuck them in at night.

60 Minutes, November 16, 2008

ON HER MARRIAGE

I married a man who came from a very different kind of upbringing. He didn't grow up with a father; his mother traveled the world. So we both came to this marriage with very different notions about what children need, and what does a couple need to be happy. So I had to give up some of my notions, and so did he.

Vanity Fair, December 2007

Life was you get married, you have kids, you buy a home. I thought Barack would be a partner at a law firm or maybe teach or work in the community. We'd watch our kids go to college and go to their weddings and take care of the grandkids and that was it.

People, August 4, 2008

From the beginning of our relationship there have been a lot of unexpected, wonderful twists and turns. We've affected each other's lives in pretty significant ways.

Chicago Defender, November 5, 2007

The truth is that everybody struggles with it, we just don't talk about it out loud. And then also I had to change. Because there were a lot of things time-wise that he couldn't provide, because he was not there. How do I stop being mad at him, and start problem-solving, and cobble together the resources? I also had to admit that I needed space and I needed time. And the more time that I could get to myself, the less stress I felt. So it was a growth process for me individually and for us as a couple, too.

Ladies' Home Journal, August 2008

We know we are blessed.

Campaign speech, October 22, 2008

Normal is relative. I feel like our relationship is exactly the same because we talk every night. We talk as long as we need to. So I don't feel like I'm in any way disconnected from him. So in terms of physical time together, it's more sporadic. But mentally and emotionally, it feels like we're right where we've always been.

Newsweek, March 3, 2008

There is so much work we need to do as a family and as a couple.

Sioux City Journal (IA), May 22, 2007

How do I structure my world so that it works for me and I'm not trying to get him to be what I think he should be?

People, June 18, 2007

We have very separate professional relationships, which I think is healthy.

Sioux City Journal (IA), May 22, 2007

When we married, he didn't pledge riches, only a life that would be interesting.

London Daily Mail, February 6, 2008

We do operate as individual professionals. And we're both stubborn. He has his opinions, I have mine. Just like everything else.

Chicago Sun-Times, September 19, 2004

We have a rule in our house that I can tease and he can't.

Associated Press (AP), May 29, 2007

Barack and I—as partners, as friends, and as lovers—we accessorize each other in many ways. The best thing I love having on me is Barack on my arm and vice versa, whether it's having him standing there smiling at me, or watching him mesmerize a crowd or talk to some seniors in a senior center.

Ebony, September 2008

There was an important period of growth in our marriage. He was in the state senate, we had small kids, and it was hard. I was struggling with figuring out how I was going to make it work for me. This was the epiphany. I am sitting there with a new baby, angry, tired, and out of shape. The baby is up for that 4 o'clock feeding. And my husband is lying there, sleeping. That's when it struck [me] that if I wasn't there, he would eventually have to wake up [and take care of the girls.] It worked. I would get home from the gym, and the girls would be up and fed. That was something I had to do for me.

O, The Oprah Magazine, November 2007

As individual professionals, you talk about your fears, you talk about your challenges, and you get feedback, and then you go off and make decisions based on what you think is best.

USA Today, May 11, 2007

Barack and I don't have interesting lives, never did. We're basically family people. When we go on a date, it's either dinner or a movie because we can't stay awake for both.

Chicago Sun-Times, July 1, 2008

ON THE MEDIA

This is what I haven't learned how to do. It's like I can't think out loud. I can't sort of meander through because then somebody takes a clip of the first part of the thought and twists it. What I said in the interview is, like, yeah, you know, I would want her [Hillary Clinton] to support [Barack]. I would. So I couldn't see not being enthusiastically supportive of whoever comes out of this. But that part of the interview didn't get played.

Newsweek, February 25, 2008

I've got to be careful not to be the story, because then it becomes a distraction to the broader issues.

Los Angeles Times, February 21, 2008

ON MEN

What I notice about men, all men, is that their order is me, my family, God is in there somewhere, but me is first. And for women, me is fourth, and that's not healthy.

Vanity Fair, December 2007

I think men are socialized differently. Men know how to prioritize themselves.

Naperville Sun (IL), October 18, 2004

ON MICHELLE AS ROCK STAR

I would be speaking every night of the week as the senator's wife if I tried to meet a fraction of the requests, but I don't because I just can't. I'm the parent, so when it comes to potlucks and play dates and pickups and keeping the kids on cue, that's generally me. The requests haven't died down. It's national. Sometimes I'm amazed. It's like, are you sure you want me?

Chicago Tribune, December 25, 2005

I'd get teased in my family if Barack or I started acting differently just because he's a senator. I have a big brother who would talk about us like dogs.

Ebony, March 2006

I am constantly trying to make sure that I am making him proud—
what would my father think of the choices that I've made, how I've
lived my life, what careers I chose, what man I married. That's the
voice in my head that keeps me whole and keeps me grounded and
keeps me the girl from the South Side of Chicago, no matter how
many cameras are in the room, how many autographs people want,
how big we get.

Washington Post, November 28, 2007

ON THE MILITARY

We have to remember that when our troops go to war, our families go
to war. We can do [our troops] a greater service if we can ensure that
while those folks are fighting on behalf of our country, that their houses
aren't being foreclosed on, that they have health care, that their kids
have good schools to go to. And that when they come back, maybe
they can finish their own education, or send their kids to college.

Good Housekeeping, November 2008

ON HER MOTHER

She is my salvation and not just because she is there, but because she is there in a positive way. I know that in addition to all the extra love and attention, she is instilling the discipline and the rules. She cheats a little bit as grandmas do, but the baseline in terms of how we as a family believe in instilling character and our values, I know that that's the same across the board.

Ebony, September 2008

My mother's love has always been a sustaining force for our family, and one of my greatest joys is seeing her integrity, her compassion, and her intelligence reflected in my own daughters.

One Nation speech, Democratic National Convention,
August 25, 2008

My mom does anything for us and her grandkids. All they have to do is look at her with sad eyes and she's done for. It's like, You're going to say no? You're going to tell your grandkids, "No, I'm going to stay in Chicago [instead of moving to Washington]?"

Newsweek, November 5, 2008

There's nothing like your mom. I leave assured that there's somebody there that deeply loves my girls, and understands the values that we're trying to impart. So even if she lets them stay up a little bit later than I might, or might let them not finish their vegetables every night, you know, there's still a certain expectation of who she wants them to be.

MSNBC, November 13, 2007

ON MOVING TO WASHINGTON

What will the girls need? Are they going to transition easily to the White House and this public life and a new school and a new city? I'm going to be making sure that they have their feet on the ground.

Newsweek, February 25, 2008

ON MUSIC

I'm loving Robin Thicke right now. Jill Scott. India.Arie. Love, love, love old school Lauryn Hill. I love good women who can sing, you know?

Glamour, September 2007

Stevie Wonder is my favorite person in the whole world and my favorite musician.

Ebony, March 2006

I have a pretty eclectic mix of everything, from Beyoncé to Stevie Wonder. He's my favorite artist of all time, so I probably have every song he's ever recorded. But if I hear something I like somewhere, I'll add it. I just heard this CD by Anthony David, who's an R&B guy—I put him on [my iPod.]. I also have some old Mariah Carey; the girls have reintroduced me to some of her older stuff. So I have a good mix: some pop, some R&B, some jazz.

Marie Claire, October 2008

ON OBAMA GIRL
AND BARACK'S FEMALE GROUPIES

First of all, I can't control someone else's behavior. I never worry about things I can't affect, and with fidelity, that is between Barack and me.

Ebony, March 2006

I think my husband's cute. So, you know, more power to the people who think he's cute as well.

Associated Press (AP), July 20, 2007

Barack is like Mr. *GQ* all of a sudden. He's got five white shirts and three black suits, and all of a sudden, he's best-dressed.

.   Associated Press (AP), July 20, 2007

ON OPRAH

I adore Oprah. She's just a great intellect. What she's done is that she has a broad reach. Now she can't—she doesn't convince people. I think Americans are smart enough to want to make their own decisions. But what Oprah has offered [Barack] is access to a broad base of her supporters. And what that's given Barack the opportunity to do is to just try to speak to them. So she's opened up more doors, but he's had to walk through them.

Larry King Live, February 11, 2008

ON HER PARENTS

People like my parents were happy they could get up and go to work.

Campaign speech, October 22, 2008

My parents taught me about confidence from within. Everything flows from that.

People, November 24, 2008

Growing up, my parents worked to instill a sense of pride and self-confidence in me and my brother. They taught us to work hard, pursue our dreams, and not worry about things that are beyond our control.

Marie Claire, October 2008

We had very hardworking parents. They didn't go to college, but they believed in the importance of education; they were staunch supporters of us, so we always had two parents telling us how wonderful we were.

U.S. News & World Report, February 1, 2008

ON PEOPLE WITH DISABILITIES

Seeing a parent with a disability [Michelle's father had MS] moving through the world and living life as if that disability didn't matter always made us think, What do we have to complain about? We wake up, we bound out of bed, we are healthy, we're happy, and our father is struggling to get out of bed. But he never missed a day of work, never talked about being sick. So it made it hard to wake up and say, "I don't want to go to school."

Reader's Digest, October 2008

ON HER PERSONAL PHILOSOPHY

When you're given the gift of advocacy, you don't sell it to the highest bidder.

University Wire (UWire), April 7, 2008

I am still surprised that there are people who make decisions because they're afraid of what might not work.

Los Angeles Times, February 21, 2008

My mother raised us not to make decisions on what could go wrong or we'd never go forward.

Wall Street Journal, February 11, 2008

Growing up, my mother always taught me to work hard to achieve my dreams and to never let anyone tell me that I couldn't do something. It's definitely the most valuable lesson I've learned.

Momlogic.com, July 31, 2008

The challenge for us is to ask, "What are we ready for?" This one is on us—see, we like to talk about change, but we don't really like change. We want easy change, we want change that will make us feel comfortable, but that's not how change happens; it's not something that's just going to come to you passively.

Speech, Georgetown, S.C., January 14, 2008

We are only as strong as the weakest among us.

Lewiston Sun-Journal (ME), December 13, 2007

I try to gravitate to the things that I personally am dealing with because then I can deal with them honestly and passionately, and hopefully be effective because I can relate.

Pittsburgh Tribune-Review, April 3, 2008

Our story is the great American story of success and pulling yourself up and making lemonade out of lemons.

All Things Considered, NPR, August 25, 2008

I've got my community, family, neighbors, girlfriends, my parents, people who have known us forever. And it's easier to stay grounded if the people you are surrounding yourself with really know you. You can't get too big if your mother's looking at you thinking, I know who you are.

Essence, September 2007

My piece of the American Dream is a blessing hard won by those who came before me.

> One Nation speech, Democratic National Convention,
> August 25, 2008

In America, we spend more time talking about what can't get done, what is impossible, and we pass that on to our children. We're creating a generation of doubters and kids that are timid. I don't want that for my girls.

> ABC News, January 24, 2008

Power concedes nothing without a struggle.

> *Washington Post*, February 2, 2008

ON HER PERSONAL TIME

I don't have time to watch TV. By the time I get through I'm going to hit the pillows so hard. And even when I try to watch TV, I can't keep my eyes open for one minute. And when Barack is watching TV, he's watching sports.

Larry King Live, October 8, 2008

ON POLITICS

Sometimes politics is a waste of time.

Chicago Sun-Times, September 19, 2004

Politics is a game, and it's all about mischaracterization. I don't let the game of politics influence what I say and who I will become, because in that way, this process would eat you up and spit you out, and then you look up and you won't know who you are. Barack and I made a promise to ourselves that in the end of this, no matter what the outcome, when we looked at each other in the eye, we would still be able to recognize one another. And I still recognize him.

All Things Considered, NPR, August 25, 2008

Politics is a patience game. You can't do this unless you have patience.

Newhouse News Service (NNS), August 10, 2008

Sometimes our politics uses division as a tool and a crutch. We think we can mend it all up after all the dirt has been thrown, but we can't.

Washington Post, February 2, 2008

What I like least is the gamesmanship of politics. I don't watch the debates. I don't mind being in tense situations; I just don't like watching folks in them. I never liked watching my brother's basketball games, either.

Wall Street Journal, February 11, 2008

I hate politics. This is the first time in my life that I've ever been involved whatsoever.

Campaign speech, Akron, Ohio, October 24, 2008

Barack Obama is going to fall and fall hard because he's going to have to make some decisions that people will not agree with. That's the nature of politics.

Chicago Tribune, December 25, 2005

Politics is stressful on the life of a family. You just have to keep working and try to prevent politics from drowning out the rest of your life.

Daily Princetonian, December 7, 2005

At some point along the way, you have to make sure that people are clear about who you are and the positions that you've taken because, you know, politics is as much about trying to blur the lines between candidates as it is getting to the issues.

Tell Me More, NPR, January 25, 2008

We approach politics in a lot of different ways. Barack has been told in every race that he's ever run that he shouldn't do it, he couldn't raise the money, that his name was too funny, his background too exotic. We've heard that. That's why this, this stuff now, is like, hey, here we go again, but in every instance his view, our view, has been that if you tell people the truth you can connect with people right here and now. If you can break through the noise, then people recognize the truth, that honesty does win out.

MSNBC, November 13, 2007

As a country we always wonder whether politics changes people, and one of the things we've desperately tried to do is not to allow our political lives to change who we are fundamentally.

MSNBC, November 13, 2007

There is something vicious and cynical going on and I think that most Americans are tired of it. I am talking about the state of politics and the tone of debate in this country. I think people have grown weary of this approach.

London Sunday Telegraph, December 23, 2007

I didn't come to politics with a lot of faith in the process. I didn't believe that politics was structured in a way that could solve real problems for people, so you can imagine how I felt when Barack approached me to run for state senate, I said, "I married you because you're cute and you're smart, but this is the dumbest thing you could have ever asked me to do." Fortunately for all of us Barack wasn't as cynical as I was. He knew that the American people knew better and wanted better.

University Wire (UWire), October 26, 2004

I've been very cynical and reluctant about politics. You know, politics is a nasty business, and you don't hold out hope that fairness will win, that truth and justice carry the day. You think that it's a business. And there was that part of me that said, Do we want to put ourselves out for a system that I'm not sure about?

All Things Considered, NPR, July 9, 2007

Like most people, my view about politics had been that politics is for dirty, nasty people who aren't trying to do much in the world.

Associated Press (AP), March 1, 2007

Politics is politics. And I think it's a competitive endeavor. And, you know, it's rough and tumble.

Larry King Live, February 11, 2008

ON THE PRESIDENTIAL CAMPAIGN

I hate fund-raising. Haaaaate it. Hate, *hate* it.

Newsweek, February 25, 2008

At the start of this, I said to him, "Look, baby, you can do a lot of things." He believes he can do a whole lot. If he works hard, he can change the world.

New York Times, October 28, 2008

When he announced on that cold, freezing cold day in Springfield, Illinois, in February, a year and a half ago, he stood up and he said this race never will be, never should be about him.

Campaign speech, October 22, 2008

When I go before a crowd, I'm thinking about trying to reach people's hearts.

Larry King Live, February 11, 2008

I like campaigning more than I would have imagined. This would be a hard thing to do if you didn't fundamentally like people. But interestingly enough, me, Barack, and our girls, we get energy from people. You know, when I'm tired, I get more energy coming out of a rally where I get to get hugs and I see people on the rope line tearing up because they never thought they'd see this moment. I see kids who are focused and engaged in a way that I've never seen before. That gives us both energy.

Larry King Live, October 8, 2008

There's an out-of-body kind of aspect to it.

GQ, September 2007

I'm not doing this because I'm married to him, because truly, this process is painful. If you have a choice, America, don't do this! Teach! Do something else. I tried to [tell] Barack—there are so many ways to change the world. Let's do them! I [didn't] want to run for president! Life was comfortable! It was safe! Nobody was takin' pictures of us!

Salon.com, November 28, 2007

Barack's not promising the moon. He's said all along, "This election is not about me. It's about all of us." Change doesn't happen from the top down; it happens from the bottom up. It requires everyone to work.

Minneapolis Star Tribune, October 14, 2008

I survive this stuff by not getting too far ahead.

USA Today, May 11, 2007

You know, there are two races in a presidential race. There's the race in the press, which has felt so very different from what I see on the ground. If I were just looking at the papers and not spending so much time in Iowa, I would have never predicted the outcome in Iowa.

Tell Me More, NPR, January 25, 2008

The game of politics is the thing I hate the most about this whole process.

Reno Gazette-Journal (NV), August 10, 2007

When I was a little girl, the thought of a woman or an African American being president was the furthest thing from what could be possible. So it's only now that I am seeing, in this race, these two phenomenal candidates that I know, as some have said, that we now can move beyond those issues and we can go for who we think is the best candidate.

Larry King Live, February 11, 2008

Our lives are so close to normal, if there is such a thing when you're running for President. When I'm off the road, I'm going to Target to get the toilet paper, I'm standing on soccer fields, and I think there's just a level of connection that gets lost the further you get into being a candidate.

New Yorker, March 10, 2008

It was never going to be easy.

Madison Capital Times (WI), September 22, 2008

ON PUBLIC EDUCATION

You can't just talk about improving education without talking about improving pay for teachers or making sure that parents are doing their part. People have to change their behavior in addition to systems and institutions changing.

Chicago Tribune, April 22, 2007

When you're talking about ensuring that your kids have a decent public school to go to, what's more important than that? How do you ensure that the federal government is going to invest enough resources to ensure that every single child in this country has access to a decent education?

CBS Evening News with Katie Couric, February 15, 2008

ON PUBLIC LIFE

Barack is special, and I'm willing to share him. I'm willing to share the girls. If we can have better schools and health care and help moms who are struggling and get back on track internationally, then all this? Big deal. I can handle it.

People, June 18, 2007

Being public figures was not something we planned for. This is an oddity. You just have to say, this is interesting. Being able to travel and connect with people, it's been very positive and a real blessing.

The Telegraph (UK), July 26, 2008

Our challenges get publicized, and I see that as a gift to let people know there is no magic to this.

Essence, September 2007

ON PUERTO RICO'S FUTURE

That's an issue that should be decided by the voters [in Puerto Rico].
Self-determination is a critical part of democracy.

Charleston Gazette (WV), May 15, 2008

ON RACISM

I think race is a reality of our society. . . . We've made great strides,
but we know we've got a lot of work to do. You know I can go to my
neighborhood and see race played out. It still exists. It wouldn't be
fair to say that people are making too much of it because it is still a
factor.

Chicago Sun-Times, August 5, 2007

This stuff is deep and we haven't touched it as a nation. We don't deal with pain that has been caused by racism and division. We don't deal with it. And then we're surprised when it rears its head among whites and blacks. We haven't dealt with it and it's hurting all of us. It's hurting all of us. We can't afford to have generations of children of any race believing they can't be exactly who they think they should be.

MSNBC, November 13, 2007

We're still playing around with the question of, "Is he black enough?" That's nonsense. Stop it! If a man like Barack isn't black enough, then who is?

Jet, September 2007

Race resonates all throughout the comments about my upbringing, my childhood, my access to college. It is there. Because it is me.

Los Angeles Times, August 22, 2007

ON REVEREND JEREMIAH WRIGHT

Your pastor is like your grandfather, right? There are plenty of things he says that I don't agree with, that Barack doesn't agree with. When it comes to absolute doctrinal adherence, I don't know that there would be a church in this country that I would be involved in. So, you know, you make choices, and you can't disown yourself from your family because they've got things wrong. You try to be a part of expanding the conversation.

New Yorker, March 10, 2008

The conversation Barack and I had was, This is the opportunity, this is the reason why you're here. This is why you're in this race, because there is a perspective, a voice that you can bring to this conversation that is needed and that no one else can do or say.

New York Amsterdam News, April 17, 2008

ON BEING A ROLE MODEL

We have to make sure that young men and women, boys and girls growing up, if they don't see that type of stability in their own home then they can look at some model out there, something that gives them the vision for what life can be for them. . . . The hope is that [Barack and I] offer a model.

Chicago Defender, November 5, 2007

ON THE ROLE OF FIRST LADY

People have notions of what a wife's role should be in this process, and it's been a traditional one of blind adoration. My model is a little different—I think most real marriages are.

Glamour, September 2007

Both Barack and I believe that we can have an impact in the D.C. area, you know, in terms of making sure we're contributing to the community that we immediately live in.

60 Minutes, November 16, 2008

The job depends on the time, it depends on the person, it depends on where they are in their life.

USA Today, May 11, 2007

Wow, what an opportunity. What a platform I'll have, potentially, to talk about a whole range of issues that could affect the country. What a privilege it will be to have the opportunity to speak to people's hearts, to be a part of moving this country in a different direction.

Larry King Live, February 11, 2008

There are a ton of things. It's endless what you can do in the White House. But until I get there and know what kind of resources I'll have and how much time and what's the agenda of the country, I think, truthfully, I don't know which of these many things I can focus on.

Newsweek, February 25, 2008

I don't think I can honestly emulate somebody else. I think I can only be who I can be in this role. And that's going to come with all the pluses and minuses and baggage and insecurities and all the things that I'll bring into it, plus my hopes and dreams along with it.

Newsweek, March 3, 2008

My first job in all honesty is going to continue to be mom-in-chief, making sure that in this transition, which will be even more of a transition for the girls, that they are settled and that they know they will continue to be the center of our universe.

Ebony, September 2008

It does me no good to spend my time as first lady pretending to be something other than who I am. Let's talk honestly about the challenges that we face. So that's what I bring that's unique from any other first lady. I mean, I don't know them well enough to know—I can't make that comparison but I know that this is who I am.

MSNBC, November 13, 2007

You know, I think the more that I learn about the position, there are a lot of things to do. Fortunately, I'm a great multitasker so I start sort of getting my list in order and creating order out of my life. But it's not as much overwhelming. I try not to focus on that. Because things sort of fall into place, you know? I think about the opportunity. I think about, OK, what can I do that is useful with this role?

Larry King Live, October 8, 2008

If the country needs a more traditional first lady, well I can do that. It would not emasculate me. But it wouldn't look like everybody else's; it would have a Michelle Obama flair to it, right? Because I am who I am.

Essence, September 2007

Barack and I have always been professionally independent, and I like it like that. I don't want to do my husband's job, and I don't want him to do mine. So we're focused on our day-to-day life and existence and making sure that we stay whole. And I would say that in that respect, that's where I'm his biggest adviser.

Good Morning America, May 22, 2007

I think that every First Lady in the history of this nation has brought something uniquely different and has moved that role in a fundamentally different direction. I think it has been an evolution that has gotten us to this point where I can be here, potentially to become the next First Lady, with all of my outspokenness and my approach to life and the things that I say. I think it's been an evolution in this country because of the many First Ladies that have come before.

CBS Evening News with Katie Couric, February 15, 2008

I'm going to try to be honest, funny, and open, and share important parts of me with people, hopefully in a way that will help them think about their lives and avoid the mistakes we may have made in our lifetime. What you see on the trail is probably who I will be as First Lady, because that's really who I am.

Vanity Fair, December 2007

I come to this with a lot of interesting talents. I need to be prepared to do what the country needs me to do at the time. Whether that's baking cookies or serving as a wonderful hostess, that's my job. I have to be prepared to do what's necessary. And we won't know what that's going to be until we get there. I will be staunchly invested. It is a joint project.

Associated Press (AP), May 28, 2007

Given the many skills that I have on so many different levels, I will be what I have to be at the time. And it really will depend on what the country needs, what my family needs, what Barack needs. So I want to remain flexible enough so whatever is needed of me, that's what I will do.

Good Morning America, May 22, 2007

I think that, you know, everyone who assumes the role of first lady brings something very unique to it. And it changes over time, and it's going to be affected by the situations of our time—of our generation. It impacts what the first lady's role will be. So I don't want to speculate because I don't want to box myself in and say, Well, you said you were gonna do this and now you're doing that. You know how that works. I'm not doing that.

MSNBC, November 13, 2007

I don't think in this modern society that the first lady role would be traditional because women like me are already breaking the mold.

Chicago Defender, January 30, 2008

I mean, come on. I'm an idea person. There are tons of things that I can think about doing. But I'm also a practical person. So what can you really accomplish? How much time do you have? What kind of resources do you have? What kind of staff do you have to do it? Because this stuff isn't just going to happen because you say it. How do you structure it? And what will be my other responsibilities, the things that I'll have to do?

Newsweek, March 3, 2008

I think the role of first lady is a full-time job. And my immediate priority will be to make the White House a home for our daughters. It's going to be a big change for them and they are going to need my full attention.

London Sunday Telegraph, February 10, 2008

My God, who can sit here and say, I'm ready to be president and first lady?

New York Times, May 18, 2007

ON SARAH PALIN

Governor Palin has a compelling life story, and she's certainly accomplished a great deal while also balancing raising a family. She's a working mom, so we have that in common.

Marie Claire, October 2008

A V.P. pick, it's like being shot out of a cannon. All of a sudden you're at the center of attention, and you want to look good. You're living in your home, minding your business, and all of a sudden you're on the national stage and everyone's watching.

Associated Press (AP), October 28, 2008

I think she provides an excellent example of all the different roles that women can and should play. You know, I'm a mother with kids and I've had a career and I've had to juggle. She's doing publicly what so many women are doing on their own privately. And what we're fighting for is to make sure that all women have the choices that Sarah Palin and I have to make these decisions and do it without hurting their families. So what Sarah Palin and I have that all women deserve is the choices and the resources to make their choices work.

Larry King Live, October 8, 2008

ON THE SECRET SERVICE

It's very funny watching [our] kids with the Secret Service, because these guys are really trying to be secret. And we go to places where they're trying to not look, and Sasha's like, Look, there's one. I see you. It's one of the secret people.

Campaign speech, July 8, 2007

They give us our space.

Chicago Sun-Times, July 1, 2008

ON HER SENSE OF HUMOR

I'm kind of sarcastic, and I've felt that my sense of humor had to be subjugated on some level. My husband loves my sense of humor, and we tease each other mercilessly. But if somebody doesn't get the joke, then you become a caricature of what the joke was. So it's like, Well, jeez—let me not joke, then, if it's going to be all that problematic. People get real worked up about some things I felt were really minor, funny, harmless observations about who we are as people.

Vanity Fair, December 2007

I'm really funny and fun to be around. I'm very sarcastic, it works wonders in a room when you see the movement in my face or intonation in my voice. But sarcasm doesn't translate in print. I've cut back on it, because I don't want that to be the story.

Wall Street Journal, February 11, 2008

I try to give people a broader variety of who I am so that my joke doesn't interfere with the broader point. I don't want the point to be lost because the point isn't my humor. It's not the joke. It's the actual point behind the joke. So yeah, there are times when I cut back and think about how is this gonna be perceived on paper, so that the point isn't lost.

CBS Evening News with Katie Couric, February 15, 2008

ON HER TALENTS

I can give people a perspective into Barack's character like no other person can. I mean, I'm married to the guy. I know his strengths and weaknesses, but I can also speak to his character.

Chicago Defender, January 30, 2008

I know how blessed my gifts are, because I know too many kids in my family and other communities whose futures are different because of one slip, one mess up, one thing that just didn't work out right.

Essence, September 2008

The reason I think people can connect with me when they see me and get to know me, is that I'm just not that different.

Essence, September 2008

My goal is to get people pumped up.

Jet, September 2007

ON TERRORISM

One of the things we can't do in this country is operate from a place of fear. How are we going to reestablish our footing in the world and change conversations globally so that we move to a different place in how we deal with issues of terrorism? Instead of protecting ourselves against terrorists, [we need to] build diplomatic relationships and invest in education abroad so that we're making sure that kids are learning how to read as opposed to fight us.

CBS Evening News with Katie Couric, February 15, 2008

[Terrorism is] an incredibly important concern, but where is the balance? You have to be a respected player. You have to do a little bit of both, so that nonideological, a nonfear-based approach is really what we need now as a country.

Good Morning America, May 22, 2007

ON WHAT DRIVES HER

Barack and I were raised with so many of the same values: that you work hard for what you want in life; that your word is your bond and you do what you say you're going to do; that you treat people with dignity and respect, even if you don't know them and even if you don't agree with them.

One Nation speech, Democratic National Convention,
August 25, 2008

If I died in four months, is this how I would have wanted to spend this time?

Newsweek, February 25, 2008

The world as it is just won't do. . . . We have an obligation to fight for the world as it should be. That is the thread that connects our hearts. That is the thread that runs through my journey and Barack's journey and so many other improbable journeys.

One Nation speech, Democratic National Convention,
August 25, 2008

ON WHAT SHE'D LIKE
TO CHANGE ABOUT BARACK

He would put his clothes up when he took them off. He would hang them up right away.

Rocky Mountain News, July 17, 2008

ON WHETHER SHE'LL RUN
FOR PUBLIC OFFICE IN THE FUTURE

No. Absolutely not.

Chicago Magazine, October 2004

One politician in the family is enough.

Joliet Herald News (IL), October 14, 2004

ON THE SUGGESTION THAT SHE
COULD RUN FOR BARACK'S U.S. SENATE SEAT

Ugh. No, thank you.

Newsweek, February 25, 2008

It's not because I'm not capable, but you have to have the passion for politics and the patience for it.

Naperville Sun (IL), October 18, 2004

ON WHO SHE IS

I am more than willing to share who I am and to open up my heart and soul to people so that they know that in addition to getting Barack—this tremendous mind and person to lead our country— that the people behind him and beside him, his wife and family, that we all represent what is good and wonderful about America.

Ebony, September 2008

I do best when I'm the most me that I can be. That's really all I've got. If I tried to be something different or model someone, I would get confused and it would be bad.

Chicago Tribune, December 17, 2007

The fact that I'm a vice president of a company has thrown people off. The fact that I have a career and a spouse, that I am a great speaker in my own right, some would say compelling, sends people in a tizzy at some level. But that's who women are.

Chicago Defender, January 30, 2008

I know how to bounce back from my mistakes.

AP Online, January 18, 2008

Do you think I would ever hold my tongue?

USA Today, May 11, 2007

The Michelle Obama I was last year is the same Michelle Obama I am this year. Different circumstances, same Michelle.

Newhouse News Service (NSS), August 10, 2008

I'm very much one foot in front of the other.

New Yorker, March 10, 2008

I'm one of the skeptics that Barack often talks about.

Associated Press (AP), March 1, 2007

I've got a loud mouth.

Good Morning America, May 22, 2007

I'm just trying to be myself, trying to be as authentic as I can be. I can't pretend to be somebody else.

Washington Post, May 11, 2007

Rebellion for me is articulating my views, trying to be honest about what I see. I don't think a lot of people in the public arena do that, because why are people so amazed when I do?

The Telegraph (UK), July 26, 2008

I'm still a work in progress. I think I'm 60 percent there.

Vanity Fair, December 2007

It would be hard for me to edit myself and still be me.

Marie Claire, October 2008

The values that we've grown up with, that we live and breathe, are pure American values. That is more me than the schools I went to. That is more me than the color of my skin even. That's more me than my gender.

Essence, September 2008

I'm used to doing stuff that people told me I wasn't supposed to do. That's my whole life. It's like, OK, here we go again, you know, telling me I can't do something before I even try.

MSNBC, November 13, 2007

I wear my heart on my sleeve.

Newsweek, June 30, 2008

I'm pretty convincing.

Washington Post, November 28, 2007

I know who I need to be. I've come to know myself at the age of 43. I know who I need to be to stay true to who I am and to keep my family on track. We don't always figure that out for ourselves as women.

Essence, September 2007

What I try to take into every speech is "just be yourself." And that's easy to do. As long as I don't have to be anybody other than Michelle Obama, I figure I know me better than anybody. And I can do that pretty well.

Gayle King Show, August 25, 2008

I'm a big-picture-values kind of person.

MSNBC, November 13, 2007

I am a working-class kid. I wear so many different hats in my life. The story I come out of is the story of most Americans' lives. The stuff we talked about around the table is the same. When you see your parents who don't have much getting out of bed and sucking it up every day, you learn a lot about values.

Newhouse News Service (NNS), August 10, 2008

ON WINNING THE ELECTION

To see the outcome and the emotion, it was a very emotional evening because I think people were ready to take hold of this country and help move it in a different direction.

60 Minutes, November 16, 2008

We were watching the returns and, on one of the stations, Barack's picture came up and it said, "President-Elect Barack Obama." And I looked at him and I said, "You are the 44th president of the United States of America. Wow. What a country we live in."

60 Minutes, November 16, 2008

ON WOMEN TODAY

Give yourself the space to think about who you are, who you want to be. . . . We're [always] in "do" mode. We need to be in "reflection" mode a bit more.

Naperville Sun (IL), October 18, 2004

What I talk about with my girlfriends is that before you start worrying about, "I don't have a man," where are you in your own space, in your own head? What do I need to be as healthy and happy on my own with or without? And the minute you get that in order, it seems like things fall into place.

Chicago Sun-Times, August 7, 2007

ON YOUNG PEOPLE

When you are traveling around the country, what you see is our nation in action. You see young people of all backgrounds finding their voice again, finding a reason to be excited about politics and being engaged.

Campaign speech, October 22, 2008

Politicians have kind of written young people off, maybe because of their low voter registration, their low voter turnout. You teach them that politics is relevant to their lives. When you do that, they are engaged. They are not fair-weather supporters. They don't get tarnished by a little negativity. In fact, I think that just gins them up even more.

Minneapolis Star Tribune, October 14, 2008

More and more young adults are asking questions about how their lives connect to the communities they live in. It's important for students to understand the value of contributing to their community. It's a good ethic of citizenship to instill in this generation of young people. It develops important links between the university and community.

Chicago Sun-Times, October 13, 1996

Barack's life is a good road map for young people.

Minneapolis Star Tribune, October 14, 2008

Every young person in this country should be able to go to college.

MSNBC, November 13, 2007

Acknowledgments

TOP OF THE LIST—he's probably getting tired of this by now—goes to Superagent Scott Mendel.

Next up is Niki Papadopoulos at PublicAffairs, who jumped on this companion volume to *Barack Obama In His Own Words*.

Then kudos to all the people who make sure I'm well-oiled. First, in Charleston: Jamie and Joe Wilson, John Willson and David Porter, Steve and Wendy Spitz, Ted and Pam Kusmider, and Ava, Jake, and Luke for providing me with entertainment outside my window perch, Jim Crow, Karen and Andy Norman, Kim and Brent Lhuillier, Penny Beal, Franklin Ashley, Polly Christy, Nancy Kirven, Lee Deas, Liz Rennie, Jonathan, Lauren, and Evelyn Sanchez, Seabrook Lucas, Marcia Guthrie, the Folly Beach Bluegrass Society, and the entire George Street contingent—thank you for making Ruby feel welcome!

Back in New Hampshire: Tim Ashe, Leslie Caputo, Bob DiPrete, Doc and Nancy Gerow, Dean Hollatz, Ed Leavitt, Don McKibbin, Spring Romer, Paul Rothe, Sara Trimmer, Cheryl Trotta, Andy and Donna Vinopal, and Carol West.

About the Editor

LISA ROGAK is the author of more than forty books and hundreds of newspaper and magazine articles. She has written biographies on Dr. Robert Atkins, Dan Brown, Shel Silverstein, and Stephen King. She lives in Charleston, South Carolina.